Soul Flowers

A Poetry Collection
for
Enjoyment and Reflection

Cynthia Schumacher

the Peppertree Press
www.peppertreepublishing.com

Graphic design by Elizabeth Parry

For information regarding permission, call 941-922-2662 or contact us at our website: www.peppertreepublishing.com or write to: The Peppertree Press, LLC. Attention: Publisher 715 N. Washington Blvd., Suite B Sarasota, Florida 34236

ISBN: 978-1-61493-913-9 Library of Congress: 2023917810 Printed: September 2023

Manufactured in the USA.

Dedication

For exemplary teachers everywhere
who in spite of adversity
continue to inspire their students
to become more than
they ever dreamed they could be

Special Note

Between my second and third poetry collections, I published a book titled *Butterfly Excursions* which contained 26 poems, several short stories, and some essays and sketches. Some of these poems were transferred to poetry collections which I published later. Listed below are others which are now being transferred for the first time so that they can be a part of this seventh collection.

Analogy for Heroes	Best Exit
Business Advice	Catapull
Diminutive Defenders	Grainglorious
Halloween: Scene Set	Halloween: Graveyard...
Harvest Gift	Maxim
November Notice	Pathfinder
Poet's Blessing	Romance Language
Wake-up Call	Weatherwise

Table of Contents

Soul Garden

In this garden hidden far
beyond earth and sky and star
here the lovely soul flowers grow
free from stress of sun and snow,
each one special and unique.
Should you wish to travel there
where no boundaries are known,
it may seem a pathway home
to a new world dimly seen,
strange and beautiful in dreams
where all journeys are complete.

Maxim

Greet the morning;
gather the day;
dance with the music along the way.
Then when you sense
the evening near,
bask in the magic of how and here.

Wake-up Call

Have you ever noticed how sunrise comes?
Not with a flutter and rumble of drums
but ever so quietly, shedding the night,
she bathes all the treetops in platinum light
and grants to each grass blade a glittering crown.
Edged with pale lavender clouds is her gown,
and as she glides silently into the town,
within the small houses the lamps slowly dim.
Gray sidewalks are crisscrossed with silvery trails
to mark recent passing of curious snails
intent on a stroll in the clean morning air.
New flowers are lifting their soft-petaled heads
to see if the green frogs have hopped from their beds
whle proud on a fence rail some distance away,
a rooster is strutting with arrogant stare
and trumpeting loudly, "It's day! It's day!"

Best Exit

As he departs, if you would wish him well,
no hothouse flowers need you send
to grace the rooms in which he's most at home.
Do not feel pressed to offer lavish gifts
and words of tribute or to place his name
on scrolls and plaques embellished and engraved.
Settle for simpler things. Grant him the lovely sight
of daisies white in fields of summer grass,
the song of wild birds calling to the dawn,
the swell of blue Gulf waters under which
legions of fish are hurled in shafts of silver,
the silent flow of deer through sunlit woods,
a poplar's rustling leaves and sound of rushing streams,
mountains adrift in softspun mists that rise
like tribal spirits from old Indian dreams.

Internalize and share his legacy
of quiet leadership, perceptive views,
good humor, basic loyalty,
the talent to devise solutions with creative thrust,
the wisdom to advise and nurture lasting trust.

In friendship let us part,
knowing that friendship is not limited
by boundaries of time or space or memory
but ranges free
as wind across the land,
as waves across the sea,
as music from the heart.

Nature Advisory

So often when confusion reigns in life,
one wonders what to do to cope.
It's easy to complain and yield to strife
and feel devoid of hope.
But once when winter brought confusion
to a southern clime
and January weather changed degrees
from the low twenties to six days of forty nine,
the clematis on the trellis near my garden wall
awoke to lovely warmer sunny mornings
and observed,
so this is middle winter
and spring is nowhere near.
So what! I don't do gloom.
I'll take whatever's here.
I'll bloom.

Grainglorious

Having appreciated it
    served in steaming mounds of simple sustenance
    or in the sweet stickiness of puddings
    redolent of raisins and cinnamon,
having enjoyed it closeted with pine nuts
    in the broad leaves of cabbage and of grape
    or splendid with saffron and garlic
    in the multi-mingled flavors of paella,
having found it irresistible in the languid ambiance
    of syrup swirled into crusty desserts
    or melted from fine powder into glossy glaze,
having savored it bubbling
    in a spicy fragrance of red beans and onions
    or dropped crisp and sizzling
    into warm broth of scallion and kombu,
        I must concede
        and others have agreed,
        that rice is nice.

Business Advice

If you should meet adversity,
be bold and shake his hand.
His unexpected presence
may not be what you'd planned,
but since his acumen proceeds
from confiscating lives,
by careful outmaneuvering
the best in you survives.

Romance Language

Somewhere far away in Italy,
poets sing of moonlight,
silver evenings,
dark trees against the sky,
while here on Toffaletti Street
my sister dreams,
with her elbows on the windowsill,
and waits for her boyfriend
to drive by in his yellow Pontiac
with twin speakers in the back
and bring her a pepperoni pizza.

Alternative: Maturity

Have you ever discovered
you were wrong about something
a long time ago
and you can't make it right
because anyone harmed at the time
is no longer around?
It's then you may realize all you can do
is to change and move on
so that later you'll know
that the way to perfection
is not easily found
and not a quick trip
on a multi-lane highway
but rather a tedious journey
on unpaved, narrow roads
filled with ruts and rough gravel
where the going is slow.

Catapult

When I desire Griselda's purr,
I stroke her lovely coat of fur.
She settles down upon my lap
to take a furry, purry nap.

In winter if the cold blows in,
she purring sleeps beneath my chin.
In summer when the days grow hot,
she seeks a purrfect shady spot.

Though I should travel world around
to hear how all earth's creatures sound,
no matter where I chanced to roam,
Griselda's purr would bring me home.

Retirement Party

You are a person of renown
with skills and knowledge, points of view,
with likes and loves that widely range
from hunting trips and barbecues
to college football, family ties,
homespun advice and business sense.
In short you're quite remarkable;
affection for you is immense
from those who've known you through the years.
So never think that just because
you're older now it all must end.
This age is just another time for folks
to celebrate and call you friend.

Pathfinder

Let us celebrate the learned mind,
  the kind and loving heart,
  the strong and questing spirit,
  the power to endure.
Let us celebrate fragility and strength,
  distinctive elegance and subtle wit,
  diversity, creative force, and beauty's lure.
Let us celebrate one who stood ready
  to travel new roads, to move ahead
  toward what we often were not ready to explore.
Let us celebrate one who understood
  there is always more.

Diminutive Defenders

The Fu dogs sit upon the shelf.
There wrinkled, ivory faces scan the room,
watching for strange intruders, vigilant
if they discover evil forces loom.

But cherished friends who come and go
need not seek clever methods to beguile
these small fierce guardians. When love surrounds,
the Fu dogs sleep, and in their dreams they smile.

Harvest Gift

What did you bring us, dearest friend,
to mark the summer's end?...
sheaves of ideas to help us succeed,
mounds of wise messages, options, and goals,
clusters of kindness when we were in need,
care and concern for our lives and our souls,
courage and patience to savor and share,
masses of elegance worn with a flair...
Here at this time of golden leaves
and woodsmoke rising in the crystal air,
we realize
you served us joy in flagons of loveliness
that we might drink our fill.
Because you live within our hearts,
we need not ask what bounty did you bring.
You bring it still.

Senior Moment

There are paths I've never followed,
opportunities never seen,
subjects I have not explored,
lands where I've never been.
Life can bring misdirection,
lack of focus be the cause,
and habit breed inertia
so we put our life on pause.
This can be a dangerous moment
when we need to banish doubt
and recall those childhood wonders
with so much to learn about,
when surprises came so often,
when the future gleamed ahead,
when we wanted to learn everything
and intellectually be fed.
So should you need and get the chance
to re-awake your brain,
be sure to take it quickly
or it may not come again.
There's so much more to learn and do
in the time you've left to spend,
and when you fill it joyfully,
the surprises never end.

Halloween:
Scene Set

Tread softly you who venture in the night.
Speak low.
The hollow too has visitors tonight.
Tall pointed hats are bending o'er their brew.
Upon a fence a black cat slinks,
two emerald flames for eyes.
Above my head
the starry-pebbled arch of ink-pond sky
shrinks from the many bare and twisted trees
which claw the air with broken arms.
Chill blows the breeze,
and far away a shutter knocks and knocks.
From creaking gateposts orange demons leer
with wild, triangle eyes
as if to mock the solemn popeyed owls.
The ominous ticking, ticking of a clock
invades the air,
and from the silent waters of the swamp,
white, wraith-like figures rise and glide
among the trees.
Across the yellow paleness of the moon
some see the pixies fly with caps awry.
The night is gripped in spell web,
and from knoll to grassy knoll
the goblins creep.

Halloween:
Graveyard Gourmet a la Shakespeare

Down in the holler where the green grass blows
rambles a ghost gal with more than ten toes,
tends foxfire on a rotten log,
pines for her boyfriend sunk in a bog.
Glumple, bump, swish flug, here on a hummock,
what that noise? It alligator stummick.
Dear Aunt Nellie, deep in the ground,
she rise up when she hear the sound.
Little gray ghoulies shuffle to the river;
floatin' in the swamp grass, Grandpa's flivver.
Look for a minute—Grandpa in it;
head in the engine, feet in the wheel,
oh dear Grandpa, how do it feel?
Put on the kettle, stir up the stew.
Here come kinfolks drapping from the blue.
Bubblll, bubblll, drizzle some oil,
build up the fire so the cauldron boil!
Gangrened eyeballs—throw in two,
bright red lichen, dash of home brew.
Pour in night crawlers simmered in lime,
chopped armadillo parts roasted with thyme,
polliwogs and crawfish, stingeree tail
six salamanders and one plump snail.
Hot rocks sizzle when the flame go high.
Vittles be ready in the wink of yer eye.
Ah sweet sassafras, how it smell!
How it taste? The dead don't tell!
If you wanta feast,
you gotta be deceased.

November Notice

Autumn is growing old.
The curves and hollows of the land
are covered with the brown fur of dried grasses.
Maple, sweet gum and hickory stand leafless,
their feathery tops spread like stiff fans
against the sky.
The pines alone remain to mitigate the drabness;
here and there along the slopes
evergreen bottlebrushes cluster,
unflustered by the chilly air.
In the distant call of passing geese,
in the dry mutter of rising winds,
the earth advises winter is near.
Gather what you need for home
and barn, she admonishes.
When lamplight awakes in the windows,
go inside and be warm.
Soon we will sleep under our blankets.

Analogy for Heroes

Thickets were here once,
heavy and threatening.
Thorn bushes crowded the place,
their sharp weapons mounted
like trophy beaks of predatory birds.
Dog-fennel also claimed a space,
sprawling in tangled insolence,
generating pale bloom-clusters
to lure the swirling swarms of yellow bees.
Few tried to find a passage through,
but when they did, the fight was hard.
One had to hack and batter all the way,
trying to shield the eyes, the limbs exposed,
knowing the flesh would tear, the blood would come.

Those seeing it now, this road
so smooth and wide,
who could imagine what had gone before?
On either side the meadow grass
sways gently, dandelions grow,
fences wear honeysuckle and wild rose.
Journeys are easily made.
At times a maverick storm
may hurl the dust about
and wrestle with the trees,
causing the pace to slow;
but then it's off again when all is clear—
no looking back.

Where are they now,
the ones who went before,
those stubborn, valiant souls
who cleared the way,
so that this pleasant route emerged
from land of epic wildness?
Some sleep perhaps beneath the trees
in ancient cemeteries where the stones
lie bleached and worn.
Others are lost in hidden places;
there no tombstones rise.
Dark earth and green fern shroud their bones.

Those who remain sit quietly
in shuttered rooms or on front porches
of old houses. They watch
the children play on city sidewalks
or in tree-shaded yards,
and no one is aware
of memories sunsetting in their eyes.

Before they leave us,
make sure the young sit down beside them
to learn the stories of those earlier years.
Have them roll back their sleeves
and show the long-healed scars
which mark the hardships they endured.
Let them not go from us
until we really understand
where they have been.

Memorial Contemplation

We have no need of accolades.
We have no need of fame.
A life of sharing love and joy
should be what we sustain.
Our love of God above all else,
our love of fellow man
should be the things we honor most
throughout our earthly span.
A time may come when we may learn
there was a better way
to overcome life's challenges
and gain a brighter day.
We may not always choose what's good,
we may not always understand,
but wisdom comes with trying
to do the best we can.

Garden Meditation

Here in this place where I walk,
shafts of morning sunlight glide between
tree branches, and I sense Love drifting near
in the company of bright angels
who have draped blue-blossoming vines
over the marble St. Francis standing in a corner
of the gray stone wall.

Long ago I saw a hillside
covered with morning glories,
trembling with vibrant life
as if empowered to cry aloud their beauty,
but when the day had passed,
the blue had crumpled into a shapeless sadness,
glory lost.

Still the mind remembers the loveliness of flowers
before grace had fallen from them.
Just as a fragrance possessed by memory
lingers long after,
just as the song of a moment beloved
never truly departs,
death cannot completely claim that mantle of blue.
Things dearly treasured by the soul
harbor the essence of eternity.

Now in this place, fragments reassemble—
the blue of flowersong restored,
the generous radiance of angels protecting,
the cradle of their shining hands
sheltering seeds of happiness.

Refugee

I see your picture on the cover of
a well-known magazine.
You stand next to a stolid woman,
perhaps your mother, whose gaze has
moved beyond the camera's range
as if no longer able to show interest
in the world.
But you beside her,
fifteen or sixteen possibly,
you're not the same.
You're staring straight ahead,
not sure who's staring back,
your face a mixture of emotions—
distrust and anger, fear, uncertainty—
your mouth controlled, lips clamped together,
waiting to see what the person looking back
is going to do.

I am legion,
a part of all the countless human eyes
that see you and may have some knowledge
of the chaos, terror, and great loss
you have endured.
I look at you, someone you'll never meet,
someone who'd like to be your friend,
and miles away I hope you feel me smile.
As heartless as the world can often seem,
it matters when I am aware that you exist.

Childhood Philosophy

There are angels among us I have heard grown-ups say,
so you should always be ready if they're headed your way.
If they look weak and hungry, having traveled a while,
give them something to eat and a kind sunny smile.
If their culture is different and their skin color too,
tell them you like making friends who are new.
Should angels among us happen your way,
be glad you were chosen to meet them that day.
Say you hope in the future you will see them again
at the gates of God's heaven when they call,
Come on in.

Community Project

In a small village on the front porch of a house
an old blind woman sat under the boughs
of a tall fir tree.
Christmas is coming, she called
to anyone passing by:
Come decorate for me!
Bring strings of multi-colored bulbs
that sparkle in the night.
Bring various objects to hang as ornaments
upon the branches of my tree—
lavender and golden baubles would be very nice;
others blue and silver, acorn twigs and holly berries,
velvet tassels, peacock feathers, silver tinkling bells—
I don't need to be precise.
Something that you cherish, let that be your choice.
When you come to hang these things
upon my lovely tree,
say a special blessing prayer for each you hang
to show you care
for people you will never know,
for those who can't be here.

And when the task was finished
and the old blind woman smiled,
and the tree ablaze with color
was visible for miles
against the winter sky at night,
and folks who came to see it—
the ones who helped
and others passing by
felt joy was all around—
hardly anyone noticed
that the angel at the top of the tree
was wearing dark glasses.

Weatherwise

One day I met a wise old man
while walking by the sea.
"Dark storm clouds are approaching, sir,"
I said. "Should we not flee?"

"Flee? Surely not," the sage replied.
"Please note it's almost four
and time for tea. Come join me here
beneath this cliff. I'll pour."

"But what about the lightning fierce,
the waves that swell so high,
the great surf thundering?" I asked.
"Should we all this defy?"

"How else to learn what wondrous things,"
he said, "make up a storm?
Rock-sheltered here, we'll rest as friends.
The tea will keep us warm.
Unless we face these whirling winds,
this raging ebb and flow,
unless we live with danger,
how will we safety know?"

So in this place of turbulence,
of angry wind and sea,
within this crashing chaos,
we sat secure and free
and shared the splendor of the storm
and drank a cup of tea.

...out of this nettle, danger, we pluck this flower, safety...
William Shakespeare, *Henry IV, Part 1*

Soulmate Departure

Wrap yourself in several rainbows
when you come to visit me—
what she once was will not vanish,
what she once was I still see.
All the years we knew each other
are alive in memory.
Loss and anguish are forgotten;
she's gone where she longed to be
in the beauty of God's presence,
forever loved, forever free.

Sympathy Card

Though death may walk on hillsides far,
his footsteps leave no trace.
The grass of love grows undisturbed
and fills each flattened space,
and soon birdsong and humming bees
come riding on the wind
to tell of ventures yet unseen
that wait beyond the bend.

Social Justice

Leila D. was a lady who talked to her cat.
She wore long black dresses and a very tall hat.
Some children who lived near thought her secretly rich
but odd and forbidding and maybe a witch.
They trampled her flowers, threw rocks at her cat
and once in her mailbox they left a dead rat.
Some distance away lived young Millicent Chase,
only twelve at the time, who had learned of this case.
A student of science, she hoped to become
a female detective who'd be ranked Number One.
She heard all the gossip around Leila's plight.
I must stop this, she thought, and put everything right.
I'll interview her, get the truth and make it clear
that spreading false rumors is not welcome here.
Neighborhoods should be friendly and ill will must cease.
Our town should be known as a haven of peace.

The interview happened in a very short time,
and the radio played it next morning at a quarter to 9:00.

M: Is it true, Leila D. that you talk to your cat?
L: Yes, I certainly do. What's the matter with that?
    I've learned the cat's language and he has learned
       mine.
    Whenever we chat, it's a wonderful time.

M: Second question, your hat is incredibly tall.
    Is it fashioned securely in case it should fall?
L: My long hair is coiled on my head very high.
    My hat keeps it tight; it can't loosen and fly.

29

M: Also I notice you like to wear black
    Do you find other colors will sometimes distract?
L: Yes, black seems more formal for a business affair,
    so I dress to look proper whenever I'm there.
    Also black dresses I think are the best
    when I help to serve meals at a funeral's request.
    But of course when I'm working alone in my house,
    I wear ragged jeans and an old faded blouse.
    Furthermore, if I'm needed to be publicly seen
    by the town once a year, I suggest Halloween.

M: Thank you, Leila. You've been great for this session.
L: You're welcome. I leave with a helpful impression.
    By the way, be assured that I'll never complain
    in your report today if you use my last name   .
    It's Doolittle, dear, that I'm glad to proclaim,
    since one of my relatives garnered great fame.

As all that has happened now comes to an end,
what do you think that this story portends?
Evil actions may come you can never defend,
but seeking the truth may make enemies friends.

Light Source

In the beginning before time was,
when the empty void was without shape or form,
I AM created LIGHT
for an earth evolving,
immediately seeding the universe
with incredible masses of star fire,
to bloom visibly near and invisibly far
for a newborn solar system.
Today, as we, the descendants
of all who appeared millennia afterward,
set out Advent candles
and proclaim the coming of Christmas
with a particular affection
for the spectacular brilliance
of many-colored lights,
we would do well to sense a connection
with the Creator's original presence
and long-range gift to the world.

BIRTH DAY

A story is told in a time long ago
of a couple who came to an alien land
to a place thick with dust and a floor made of sand.
The breath of farm animals seasoned the air
as the man gathered straw to establish a place
for his wife to recline and to wait for the time
for her child to be born in this limited space.
Her body was heavy, her steps very slow.
Long hours of travel had made tiredness grow.
She's so young, he worried.
She may need special care.
If she rests now, she might rebuild strength before dawn.
Though the inn gave no lodging,
perhaps they might share
one of their servants to come later on.
Once she is sleeping, I'll return to the inn,
only minutes away, to find who they can send.

He secured the large doorway and found a place near
    one wall
to watch through the night hours in case she should call.
But fatigue is persistent and he soon fell asleep
and slumbered so soundly he heard nothing at all.
When he wakened much later, a lantern hung near.
Its glow filled the place he had made for his wife,
who was still present and had suffered no harm,
but now its appearance was changed from before.
Spotless and gleaming was this once dusty space
where she rested smiling, dressed in garments of white,
holding the baby asleep in her arms.
He gazed in amazement. How could this be?
His mind filled with shame as his heart surged with joy.
He had slept through the birth of this beautiful boy!

He stammered and stuttered and tried to explain,
but she showed only affection when she spoke his name:
All is well, my dear Joseph. We are blessed indeed.
God loves us and gave us this wonderful child.
He has brought us so many remarkable things.
He sent us the helpers you thought I would need.
I had nothing to fear and I never felt pain.
Their voices were music that sings in the wind.
Their hands soft as flowers that welcome the spring.
I could not see faces, but I know they had wings.

Then she paused and said, *Listen.*
I think there is more.
I hear someone coming.
Go open the door.

Best Wishes

...so easy to express in words said or sent
during this time of the year
when religious and secular advocates
of ancient rituals and festive affairs
celebrate the season,
when ribbons of color—red and green,
silver, blue purple, and gold—
dazzle the eye in stores and houses,
glow in evenings underneath the stars.

Now in these jolly, jubilant days
when generosity is in style,
bestow these wishes frequently
to one and all you meet
because it is the popular thing to do.

But when night comes and all is still,
send more,
wrapped in cocoons of honest prayer,
to people you will never know,
to those with blighted lives who suffer much
and often die in a harsh, indifferent world.
Wish for them peace, so that when all is ended,
their souls will rise, brighter than starbirth,
from earthly husks devoid of breath and animation
and speed beyond parameters of time and space
toward the indescribable joy
of infinite love.

Mary Pondering

When he was born, he was so beautiful.
Beyond that moment she could not visualize
the years ahead but felt only all-consuming joy.
As he grew older, developing from child to taller youth,
his quiet wisdom sometimes glimpsed by
local citizens and learned men,
she wondered often how his life would be
when he became a man mature and self-assured.
She did not mind in later years when he
left home to share his views with other folk
and go where he believed God led him.
She saw him less but knew his love
for her would always be the same.
She understood why others sensed his worth
and felt compelled to follow him.
When in his prime he died, unjustly vilified,
she thought of Simeon who long ago had said
a sword would pierce her heart.
Sharing the agony upon his face before his death,
she feared she would continue haunted by this sight.
Those closest to her counseled her:
Be not distressed. You are our mother now.
The violent pictures in your mind will someday fade.
Sad memories will diminish and only happiness remain.

It did not happen quite that way,
Instead she learned that ever after those she met,
no matter whether young or old, became her kin,
for when she looked at them,
she always saw His face in theirs
and they were beautiful.

Poet's Blessing

As you walk through the world,
may the grass be green.
May you feel the presence
of angels unseen.
May you sing among roses,
be kissed by the wind,
and believe that your journey
will happily end.

Postscript

When I first began writing poetry during my high school and university years, I had no idea that I would finally plan to preserve my work once I retired. Since I had never pursued a writing career, I decided to self publish my poetry as the easiest way to keep track of it. This began in 1988, at a time when relying on companies that set type and used a printing press was the best option for me to consider. It was a labor-intensive process involving contacting the copyright office in Washington, DC, in order to protect my work.

Although I found enjoyment in having enough copies to sell to family, friends, and acquaintances or to small groups that enjoyed my poetry talks about the importance of poetry's influence in history and on the lives of many individuals personally, I discovered an unexpected future audience for poetry in the modern world. I discovered that many people who responded positively to my writing seldom read poetry or purchased poetry books in their everyday lives. For this reason I was happy that I had taken the time to begin publishing my poetry collections throughout the remainder of my life. I have also continued encouraging people to learn ways to explore poetry so that they might be tempted to write poetry themselves.

This book is the seventh of my poetry collections. Several earlier collections arrived during years when printing companies finally had computers to use themselves: however, I had no access to a personal computer of my own. I still have copies of each of the first five collections, but they will always be considered out of print. In the intervening years the world has changed greatly and now my sixth and seventh collections will be available for my readers to order online. Now also more and more people have had their poetry professionally recognized and published for others to purchase.

When I chose to pursue a public education teaching career, I always tried to encourage students to become familiar with poetry and to appreciate its value as a way to enjoy the use of language. In my talks with adults about how to read and understand the ways to experiment and enjoy the rewards of trying to write poetry, I encouraged them to think about their own lives and to reflect on methods of putting into words the things that meant the most to them.

Throughout the world there are many wonderful teachers who have influenced students to love learning One of them taught me many years ago to love poetry. That is why I have been writing it for 78 years. In sharing my work with others, it has always been my hope that among those who read it will always be some who discover those universal thoughts and emotions expressed that are common to humanity and that may often cause us to feel a kinship with other writers across the ages.

Other Books by the Author

Poetry Collections
Polished Stones
Firefly Encounters
Wellspring Legacies
Soul Candles
Creekstone Crossings
Seeds from Wild Grasses

Books for Children
Colorful Character
Searching for S
Willenbron and the Gralumpy

Fairytale Musical in Pantomime: *Rapunzel*
(Script: songs, music, narration, dances)

Cynthia Schumacher is a retired public school teacher and a part-time educational consultant on constructive approaches to teaching and learning. She lives in Sebring, Florida.

Printed in the USA
CPSIA information can be obtained
at www.ICGtesting.com
JSHW042255020724
65612JS00012B/1